THE
Archive Photographs
SERIES

HARPENDEN
THE SECOND SELECTION

The Harpenden Sign, erected in May 1937.

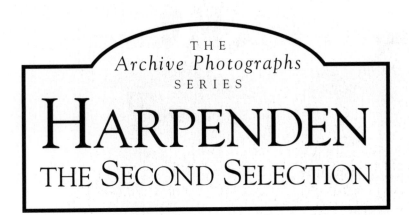

THE
Archive Photographs
SERIES

HARPENDEN
THE SECOND SELECTION

Compiled by
Eric Brandreth

CHALFORD

First published 1997
Copyright © Eric Brandreth, 1997

The Chalford Publishing Company
St Mary's Mill, Chalford,
Stroud, Gloucestershire, GL6 8NX

ISBN 0 7524 1003 2

Typesetting and origination by
The Chalford Publishing Company
Printed in Great Britain by
Bailey Print, Dursley, Gloucestershire

Dedicated to Sheila and Paul,
in appreciation of their encouragement.

Contents

Waverley Mills in 1923, formerly the Brewery.

Introduction

A hundred years ago in 1897, when part of the St Nicholas building estate behind the church was to be auctioned, the brochure, reasonably enough, went to great lengths to emphasise the attractions of its location.

It read: 'Harpenden is a charming village, five miles south of Luton, five north of St Albans, and twenty-four and a half from London, in the county of Hertford, one of the prettiest and most interesting of the Midland counties. The village lies four hundred feet above the level of the sea, has a gravel soil, with a subsoil of chalk, and is exceptionally bracing, fogs being very seldom experienced in the district. The surrounding country is very beautifully undulated and well timbered, and its scenery is unsurpassed in the county. The village is lighted with gas, and the water supply is excellent. Probably nowhere else within so short a distance of London is there a spot so absolutely rural, picturesque and healthy. There is a station in the centre of the village on the main line of the Midland Railway.'

Thirty years later, in 1928, when several areas were being developed, Jarvis's brochure for the Carisbrooke Estate described Harpenden as 'the place in the sun' and said: 'Its popularity as a residential neighbourhood has considerably increased since the war, owing to its accessibility to London: there is an excellent service of fast trains, some of which take only thirty-five minutes for the journey. The fact that at present there are no less than 1,400 season ticket holders (from a population of just under 9,000) speaks for itself. Harpenden is very convenient for businessmen.'

In 1928, a three monthly season ticket to St Pancras cost £8 8s 9d (£8.44) for first-class, or £5 9s 3d (£5.46) for third class.

The train is still important to Harpenden. In 1991 2,230 people regularly went to work by train, mostly to London. But another form of transport is creating problems. Over 8,000 people went to work by car: with 524 cars per 1,000 population, Harpenden has one of the highest ratios of car ownership in the country. Hertfordshire County Council has just published a Transportation plan for Harpenden, which says 'In recent years there has been a growing awareness across the country that our transport system is becoming out of balance with the nature and needs of our communities. There is in Harpenden a public perception that although the standard of living has increased over the last thirty years, the quality of living has deteriorated.'

The plan aims to reverse this situation, by reducing the adverse effect of heavy traffic within the town, and thus restoring and maintaining the wealth of assets, both natural and man-made, which make it such a pleasant place.

The pictures in this book show some of these assets, and the ways in which they have changed; and also give a glimpse of the quality of life over the years.

One

In the Beginning

The first documented reference to Harpenden dates from 1221, when a Papal Bull mentions St Nicholas church as a chapel of ease to the mother church, St Helen's at Wheathampstead. But people had lived here long before that. Harpenden lies in a dry valley, between two river valleys, the Lea and the Ver. Over two thousand years ago these rivers were wider and deeper, and navigable. The natural vegetation of the area is deciduous forest: with the exception of the gravel and sand deposits in the river valleys, the land was covered with dense woodlands. Early men came to the region from north-west Europe, via the Thames and the River Lea. These were the Belgae: they moved inland from the river banks, clearing small sites for settlements, which we still know as 'Ends' and 'Greens'. Traces of their occupation have been found at Coldharbour. They were followed by the Romans, who founded Verulamium a few miles away, and created a network of roads, one of which, linking Dunstable with Cheshunt, passed through Harpenden, along what is now the northern end of the A1081, and then along the ridge from Cooters End to Aldwickbury, and on to Wheathampstead. The Romans were in England for four hundred years, and artefacts from their time have been found at several sites in Harpenden.

These are the remnants of the oldest man-made building in Harpenden. They stand on private land at the top of the Rothamsted Estate and were excavated in 1937 by A.W.G. Lowther. This was a small Roman shrine and a circular building in the centre contained a life sized statue of a God looking out to the east. Around this was a rectangular wall of flint, with an outside ditch. Three cremation urns were found within the rectangle; they were dated to the early years of the second century AD.

In the 1820s a tumulus at Coldharbour, twenty feet high and fifty feet around the base, was opened. Inside was this Romano-Celtic sarcophagus. It had been hewn from a gritty calcareous stone, and consisted of a circular, hollowed out tub-like coffin, two feet high and three feet in diameter, sandwiched between two slabs, each five feet long by three feet wide, and a foot thick. Both were broken into two during excavation.

Inside the coffin were five objects denoting the site of a human burial. One was a square jar with a reeded handle. It was made of pale green glass, and was about fifteen inches high. It contained human remains. With it were four shallow earthenware dishes, of a type commonly used to hold offerings of food and drink for the departed one's journey. These objects were dated to about 150 AD. They were donated to the British Museum in 1844.

Puddingstone is a natural conglomerate of pebbles cemented by silicate into a very hard rock, and is fairly widespread across Hertfordshire. It was formed in Eocene times about 60 million years ago, when much of Southern England was under the sea. Some people believed that it continued to grow. In the early 1900s, Charles Bigg, a worker at Rothamsted, determined to test this. He washed, dried and weighed three stones, bound them with copper wire to identify them again, and buried them, intending to dig them up in ten years time to see. Unfortunately he died and no-one else could find them again.

The groundrock of Hertfordshire is chalk. It is not a very good building stone, as it weathers badly, but in the past was often used, as no other stone was available. Here it is seen in a local building, used in conjunction with puddingstone and flints, which, being much harder, gave some strength to the wall.

During the construction of the Great Northern Railway through Coldharbour in the late 1850s, workmen discovered some early Iron-age fragments. Unfortunately, some of them were damaged before it was realised what they were. But still in good condition were two bronze bucket handles, of which this is one. Each had an escutcheon, moulded as a ram's head. The nostrils were enamelled in a deep vermilion colour, which was still in almost perfect condition. They were presented to Luton's Wardown Museum in 1928.

Two
The Village Centre

Until about the third decade of this century, the High Street had a much more rural appearance than it does today. Three farmhouses, two breweries and several inns rubbed shoulders with domestic cottages. A small stream ran alongside the lower High Street. Small shops, usually in one room of the cottage, sold only the basic necessities of daily living. The blacksmith, wheelwright, saddler, ropemaker and other craftsmen who supplied the needs of an agricultural village were mainly located between Station Road and Sun Lane. During the inter-war years only three or four shops were not privately (and locally) owned. This began to change in the mid-1930s, when Woolworths, Boots and Sainsburys were built on the old Waverley Mills site. The last major building work in the High Street was in 1970, when the new Sainsburys was built. In the last decade, building activity has been concentrated on Vaughan Road. But the High Street is not only Harpenden's main shopping area: it is also the main road between Luton and St Albans and as such carries a very heavy load of traffic. The daily traffic flow has doubled in the past twenty years and now averages 22,500 vehicles per day. At peak hour 2,250 vehicles pass through the High Street; fifty per cent of that is through traffic, with neither origin nor destination within the town.

The Railway Hotel, c. 1895 (now the Harpenden Arms). James Mardall, owner of the Peacock Brewery, had it built in about 1870, replacing an old shack. The landlord in 1890 was Richard Longland, who had many interests. He was a wine and spirit dealer, a corn and hay merchant, and had livery stables in Station Road behind the hotel. He was also managing director of the Harpenden Gas Company. The building on the right, no. 2 Southdown Road, is part of an old medieval hall building, dating from about the fifteenth century.

The High Street seen from a window of the Railway Hotel around the turn of the century. The cart on the left is a Midland Railway one, delivering passengers' luggage, according to the caption on the hood.

Harpenden Motors site, next to The George, *c.* 1975. They had been there since 1954, when they took over from Chirneys, but closed down in 1983. The site has been empty and unused since then. During the last war the WVS opened a canteen there for members of the ATS. They appealed for donations of carpets, cushions, tables, chairs and other home comforts. They were given all of these, together with a piano and a radio, known in those days as a wireless.

The Finchley Ladies hockey team stayed at The George while on tour in 1908.

The High Street, early morning, c. 1905. The trees on the right were considered an obstruction to traffic and were removed in 1935.

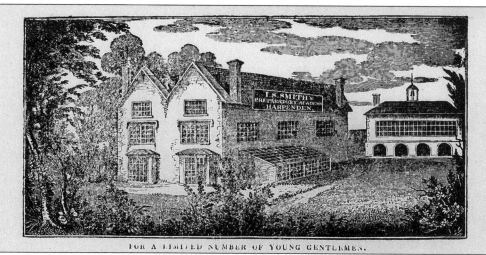

FOR A LIMITED NUMBER OF YOUNG GENTLEMEN.

Thought to date from around 1830, this engraving of John S. Smith's Preparatory Academy for a limited number of young gentlemen puzzled the Local History Society when it was discovered by one of their members at the Bodleian Library in 1987. Following the few clues there were, and checking with the 1843 Tithe Award, Eileen Haines identified it, and placed it as the house standing at the corner of Church Green. She also traced an 1886 sales notice for the house, which confirmed the location. The schoolroom at the back appears to be artistic licence.

Island Cottage, *c.* 1885, the same building as that depicted in the engraving above. The house is just visible behind the tree in the garden at the corner of Church Green. It was offered for sale in 1886. By 1890 it had been demolished and the shops, which are still there now, built. One of them became Skillman's (see opposite).

Postmaster Daniel Barton Skillman with his staff, *c.* 1903. The shop is now Forbuoys. The post office had been here since 1898: in 1905 Daniel Skillman and it moved to the Lower High Street (see p.28). As well as being postmaster he was a cycle agent, a stationer and an insurance agent for four separate insurance offices, covering life protection, accidents, fire, burglary and housebreaking and plate glass damage.

Shops in Leyton Road in 1970. From left to right are: Ian Breed, hairdresser; Godshaw, jeweller; and Stephen Sander, electrical appliance dealer. Also pictured is The Birdcage, ladies outfitters. The first three shops were demolished in 1989 and the Leys shops were then built, with a covered walkway through to the High Street.

West's bakery at about the turn of the century. Joseph Edwin West was born in 1859 at Turvey in Bedfordshire. As a boy he joined the Royal Navy, where he was trained as a baker. He came to Harpenden in 1897 and established his business here. These premises were rebuilt in 1912; they are now an estate agents. Joseph West retired in 1932 and died twelve years later.

This baker's oven, made by H. Smith and Son of Lambeth, was installed in 1905. It had an arched brick roof, and stretched back several feet into the wall. Although not used from about the late 1960s, it was not removed until 1982, when Barclays Bank was extending at the rear of the building.

These seventeenth-century cottages faced Church Green until 1959. They were then demolished and replaced by shops, including Harpenden's first supermarket, with flats above. Two rooms in the end cottage on the right were rented in the 1860s by the Harpenden Lecture Institute and Reading Club for use as a reading room.

The Parish Church and part of the churchyard, c. 1905, showing two wooden 'bedhead' memorials. In the eighteenth and nineteenth centuries these were common in this area, which has no suitable local stone. The wood deteriorates with age and a few years ago the last remaining 'bedhead' memorial was removed for preservation.

There is a timeless quality about this picture. Probably taken in about 1880, it could represent almost any time in the last century; the High Street would have changed very little. Early in this century two swans lived on the pond. One was accidentally run over and given to the Common Keeper for disposal. He was on the Rothamsted Allotment Club Committee and their annual dinner happened to be due. That year the members dined on roast swan, rather than their usual side of beef.

The same view in winter, with a splendid slide across the frozen pond.

Sun Lane on 24 April 1908. Snow was rather late that year. Harpenden has the odd cold spell from time to time. Perhaps the record occasion was in 1963, when, from 16 to 24 February, the temperature was permanently below freezing point: at its peak on the 23rd, the thermometer reached 2° Fahrenheit, thirty degrees of frost.

The northern end of the High Street in August 1959. The cottages fronting Church Green can be seen on the left, behind the trees. Doris Crouch's wool shop, with the Plumbers Loft behind, is just to the right of the Old Cock Inn. In 1973 a town centre plan was published. In order to alleviate traffic problems, it proposed two new service roads, to run behind the shops on each side of the main road. Rather optimistically it said that these proposals were perfectly capable of implementation by 1981.

Doris Crouch's woolshop has already gone and the Plumbers Loft is being demolished in 1972. The small building on the left was W.T. Smith's, the corn merchants and garden supplies shop.

The buildings were replaced by this block of shops with offices above. The small shop to the right was Rowe's bakery (see p.101).

This building, now S and N Interiors, was erected in about 1921. Before it on the site was The Leather Bottle, a public house from about 1870 to 1920. In 1935, when it was decorated for King George V's Silver Jubilee, it housed Frank Bentley, decorator, Fred Timson, general outfitter and bootmaker, and Thomas Chambers, a hairdresser who also repaired umbrellas.

Immediately to the left of the building above was Sally Bonfield's cottage. The small porch was said to be her living room. The cottage behind was demolished at about the same time as The Leather Bottle, leaving the porch as a tiny island cottage (see next picture). Fred Timson had taken it over in 1919, the date of this photograph, and Alf Fellows, who worked for him, repaired boots and shoes there.

Putterills the Motor Engineers acquired the site behind the island cottage in 1935 and established their workshops there. Their main garage and showroom was on the other side of the High Street. They coped with this restricted entrance for many years, but in 1956 the small building was demolished. When Fred Timson retired in 1948, Alf Fellows carried on the business. Displaced in 1956, he moved into premises in Bentley's yard, behind the building just visible on the right.

Rose Cottage in 1965, at that time the last residence in the High Street. The roses had been planted in 1950 by Paddy McCoard, the owner. Every summer they made a beautiful display of colour. The building is now Alan Bramwell's dental surgery.

Broadway Parade shops being demolished in April 1969, to make way for Abbey National. In 1840 this was the site of Bowers Farm. St Dominic's School started in Bowers Cottage, which had been the farmhouse, in 1920. They outgrew it and moved to Harpenden Hall three years later. Bowers Cottage was then bought by Jesse Catton, who demolished it and built the shops, which opened in 1926.

Jesse Catton also built Broadway Hall, the covered market, in the gardens behind the original cottage. It opened on 15 April 1933 with sixteen shop units. In 1940 the Army requisitioned the building and used it as a catering stores depot throughout the war. It was transferred to the YMCA for a similar purpose in 1945. It was given back in September 1953, as seen here. The market reopened shortly afterwards, and continued until it was demolished in 1968. Sainsburys now occupies the site.

Brewery House, *c.* 1950, when it was still a private home. It had been built in 1871 by James Mardall, who owned the Brewery. The house was sold in 1951, together with nearly three acres of land, which reached up to the railway line, and was converted into shops and offices. W.H. Smith and Going Places are there now.

The Brewery House gardens in September 1926. Beyond the garden hedge is part of Brewery Meadow and beyond that the railway line. W. H. Smith's shop now extends across the garden and at the far end is the elevated approach to Sainsbury's car park.

Harpenden Post Office in the Lower High Street in September 1928. It had been here since 1905 and in 1928 was about to transfer to the newly built office in Station Road. This building was then taken over by a firm of butchers, the Empire Meat Company, who put in a redesigned shop front, with picture windows. It later became Dewhurst, which closed down in 1991. It is now Margies, selling camping equipment.

No. 9 Vaughan Road in 1985. It was for many years the home of Arthur Edward Anscombe, son of Allen Anscombe, founder of the department store in Leyton Road. Arthur was the architect who designed the Congregational church (see opposite), built in 1897. He is also believed to have designed this house. It was built in 1912; he became the first owner and was still living here in 1940. By 1950 it was serving as offices for Jarvis's building firm. The house was demolished in 1986.

A postman and telegraph boy moving equipment to the new post office. In 1890 the post office was where the Manor Pharmacy is now. Mail was brought to it from St Albans in a pony cart. The driver delivered to houses on his route; he blew a whistle warning the cottagers to come out and collect their letters. There were then four postmen to cover the area. When they moved into Station Road there were twenty-three.

The Congregationalists met at their chapel in Amenbury Lane from 1840 until the 1890s. In 1894 they decided to build a new church, as the existing one was too small and inconveniently situated. There were cowsheds next door. They bought a plot of land along Victoria Road, fronting Station Road, but quickly exchanged it for a cheaper one backing on to it, which faced Vaughan Road. This church opened on 3 March 1897, before the northern side of Vaughan Road was developed.

Mardall House in January 1988, just after completion. It stands on the site of Arthur Anscombe's house (see p.28) and is named after the Mardall family, who in the last century owned the brewery and the land. When the Brewery closed in 1919, it became the Waverley Mills, and this area was Jarvis's yard. In 1972 they built the small building on the left, which was used as an office.

These buildings were the Brewery stables. Jarvis's adapted them for a machine and joinery shop. The space at the far end of the yard was their timber store. When Jarvis transferred to Batford in 1987, these buildings were used by S.D.S. Media Print and the small offices by Harpenden Glass. The whole area was cleared early in 1997, in order to prepare the site for the new police station.

The top entrance to the Brewery cellars in January 1997, now underneath the car park end of the new police station. The main entrance was behind the Brewery tower, where Boots is now. Used for storing the newly made beer in cool conditions, the cellar had railway tracks laid, on which the barrels could be rolled more easily. It was about 75 feet long by about 17 feet wide. At this end there were 29 steps up to ground level.

In April 1942 Jarvis's allowed the Home Guard to set up a rifle range in the cellar. The planks were put up at the end as a safety measure and it was well used for the next few years.

In April 1947 the Public Library, which had been in a room at Harpenden Hall for over ten years, moved into the Victoria Road School. This had become vacant at the end of the Second World War, when the First Aid Emergency Post closed. Harpenden then became the first County Branch Library to have a separate, specially designed, children's room. This picture shows a Saturday morning story hour in May 1947, when there appears to be rather more formality than there is nowadays.

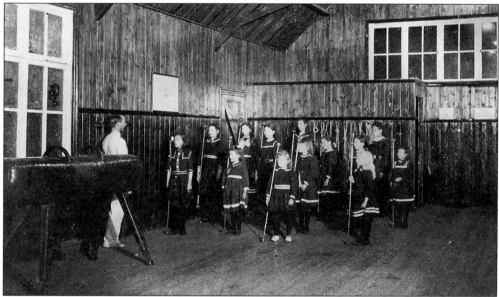

On the other side of Vaughan Road was the gymnasium, erected in about 1901. The club had been meeting in the old infant school in Leyton Road, but when the Urban District Council took over the fire brigade, that building was needed for them. Mr Tylston Hodgson of the Welcombe provided this building. The club, with an ex-army man as instructor, had separate evenings for boys and girls. Parents and prospective members were invited to witness a meeting before deciding whether to join. In the early '30s, this building became the School of Dance and Elocution (see p.117).

Three
Both Sides
of the Common

At the southern end of the High Street, before the Bull roundabout was built, the road forked, leading to Hatching Green on the right, and to Southdown on the left. In the middle of the last century these were two small hamlets, separated from Harpenden, and each other, by the 238 acres of the gently rising Common, covered with gorse, which stretched away for more than a mile to the south. Hatching Green was, in those days, a small cluster of cottages around the green. There was an inn, the White Horse, which dates from the seventeenth century. A carpenter had his workshop and sawpit there and across the road was Hatching Green Farm. Rothamsted's main entrance led off the green. At the outbreak of the First World War a temporary tented military hospital was set up just inside the gates; it moved into the golf clubhouse when colder weather came. Southdown, then known as Bowling Alley, had in 1851, only 48 houses. 245 people lived there. When the Midland Railway extension to London was being planned, a large area of land for it was bought from Limbrick Hall farm. When the line was completed the surplus land was sold, and, by 1871, 98 new houses were built along Grove Road and the newly extended Cravells Road.

The Dell, Harpenden Common.

This card was posted in 1912. The road beyond the pond is Wheathampstead Road, renamed Southdown Road in 1924. The Brickle Dell was dug out in the eighteenth century, when clay was taken to make bricks. Mrs Tylston Hodgson of the Welcombe (now the Harpenden House Hotel) had the fir trees planted towards the end of the last century to improve the view.

Bowling Alley in about 1860, as painted by Jane Gilbert. This was eight years before the Midland Railway came. The white building in the centre is Patmores Farm in Queens Road and the row of cottages on the right was known as 'Physic Row' having been built by Dr Kingston in the early years of the century. The small pond seen in the previous picture is just visible on the left.

Harpenden Gas Company was formed in 1864 at Southdown, supplying gas mainly for domestic use: street lighting did not begin until the 1880s. There was a showroom in the office building to the right of the entrance until 1956. In the beginning, gas was made on the site, but later it was made elsewhere and stored here. The UDC bought the site and in 1964 demolished the outbuildings, (but not the gasholders) and created the Southdown Industrial Estate, seen here in the late '60s.

34

Southdown, c. 1960. The area has seen many changes: Broadstone Road has since been built across the field at the bottom and Sherwood Rise has been built down the middle of the allotments in the centre. Across the road is the Grove School building site; the school opened in 1964. Towards the top of the picture on the left is the Rugby Club ground at the end of Overstone Road. The club moved to Redbourn Lane in 1964. The fields to the right are now covered by Aldwickbury Crescent and Alzey Gardens. The buildings along Southdown Road, just below the gasholders, were redeveloped in 1980, when the Finefare supermarket (now Somerfields) was built.

Piggottshill Lane being widened in 1930. The houses on the left are in Barnfield Road. Houses were built on both sides of Piggottshill Lane during the '30s, displacing some of the allotments which can be seen on the right, although most of them still remain. Two adjoining houses which were built on the right hand side were requisitioned in 1939 almost immediately after completion, and used by a team of military dentists throughout the war.

The Rose and Crown was built during the 1860s, when the area was expanding rapidly. The first landlord was Thomas Vine, who worked there from 1870 till his death in 1882. His widow then carried on for another eight years. In 1908 William Hysom was the licencee and he remained for about thirty years. The name Rose and Crown commemorates the marriage in 1486 of Henry VII to Elizabeth of York, which united the houses of York and Lancaster.

Piggottshill Lane at about the same time as the picture opposite, looking downhill. The tree on the right is the one seen there at the end of Barnfield Road. There were many steam rollers still in use in the 1950s.

An old cottage at Hatching Green in 1928. The home in the 1890s of Betsy Peacock, it was known to the young lady who took the photograph as 'the witches' cottage'. It was demolished long ago. The building on the site now is Hatching Hall.

A group of pictures of the Grove, at the far end of Grove Road, in 1928. It is an early eighteenth-century house, with later additions. In 1744 the house belonged to the House family, owners of the Peacock Brewery in the High Street. In 1907 the Grove passed to a nephew, Charles Francis Sibley (see p.80). He moved here from Annables, and farmed the 1,000 acre estate until 1928, when he moved to Pipers in semi-retirement. He died there four years later aged 76.

Charles Sibley gave half a century of public service to Harpenden. He was born at Annables, Kinsbourne Green, in 1856 and grew to be described as 'a fine figure of a man', weighing around 24 stone. He was a manager of Kinsbourne Green School, opened in 1869, which his father had helped to build. He was also one of the two Vestry stone-wardens, who were responsible for the maintenance of the parish roads.

Charles Sibley was elected to the St Albans Rural District Council on its formation in 1894 and was its chairman three times. He was a member of the Board of Guardians, looking after the welfare of the poor, from 1895. For many years he was a trustee of Harpenden United Charities. He was also chairman of Harpenden Races Committee for nearly thirty years, organising the horse racing on the common. Elected to the County Council in 1913, he served until 1928, when he did not seek re-election.

Despite his great record of public service, Charles Sibley was remembered by many as the man who tried to close a public footpath in December 1913. The path ran from Crabtree Lane, opposite what is now Gilpin Green, to Pipers Lane, across his land. He had both ends fenced off and, despite opposition, the path remained closed for a week. But the following weekend a large gathering of people, led by Spencer Pickering of The Granary, forcibly removed the railings and broke through on to the path. After discussion, it remained open. The Grove now belongs to Craigmyle and Co., a firm of fund raising consultants.

Rivers Lodge at about the turn of the century. It is an early eighteenth-century building and an extension on the right hand side was built in 1914. This was the home from 1872 of Thomas and Jessie Wilson, where they raised a family of four boys and three girls. In 1885 their nursemaid left suddenly. Theodora, who, at seventeen, was the eldest child, was in her element, 'washing and dressing, cutting bread and butter, washing up and making beds, just what I do enjoy. It was such a pleasant week'. The parents then went to Tunbridge Wells and returned with little Milly 'only 14, but a dear little thing'.

Thomas Wilson was born in 1841 at Highbury. He read for the Bar, but, as his health was not good, did not follow a legal career. Shortly after leaving Cambridge, he became tutor to the two sons of Lord Tennyson, the Poet Laureate. In 1872 he married and came to Harpenden shortly afterwards. His wife was a cousin of Dr Gilbert. Thomas Wilson was a keen linguist and worked at Rothamsted as a translator. He was also interested in meteorology and kept various instruments on a stand in his back garden, seen above.

The small sitting room at Rivers Lodge, *c.* 1890, showing the Adam-style work on mantelpiece, alcove and ceiling. Thomas Wilson died in 1915. When Jessie Wilson died in 1926, there were only two daughters still living at home. Their architect brother, Dennis, had a house built for them (see p.65). Rivers Lodge was bought by Rothamsted but, as it was not immediately required, was let to Captain Bulger for seven years. He was a keen huntsman, and had the outbuildings restored to their original use as stables. Rivers Lodge is now part of the Rothamsted Experimental Station buildings.

The Rothamsted Director's house, in about 1913, when Sir John Russell was the director. This house was demolished in 1925 and the present one built. Behind it there was a very large garden. A few years ago this was developed with prestige housing, known as Waterglades, Sir Joseph's Walk, West Common. It should, of course, logically be Sir Henry's Walk. Although the first director's name was Joseph Henry Gilbert, he was never, throughout his life, known as Joseph. He was Doctor Gilbert until his knighthood in 1893 and, from then on, always Sir Henry until his death on 23 December 1901.

One of the pair of ancient cottages situated behind the Silver Cup was the home of Mrs Mary Constable. When she was born at Bowling Alley in 1810, there were only thirteen houses there. She came here when she married and lived here until she was 92. She was a straw plaiter from a very young age until she was 60 and regularly took her plait to St Albans' market, thinking nothing of walking there and back. These cottages were demolished in 1902. She moved to the Old Bell district and died there ten years later, at the age of 102.

This engraving dates from the early nineteenth century. Heathfield Lodge, standing behind the old cottages above, was built as a residence for Thomas Reynolds, son of the rector, in the mid-eighteenth century. From 1805 until 1856 it was let to James Wyatt, a barrister, known in Harpenden as Counsellor. Every Sunday he walked to the Parish Church, preceded by his foot-man, who carried his prayer book. In the 1870s it was Field's Hat Factory. When they moved to Southdown in 1883 it became Abbott, Anderson and Abbott's, oilskin manufacturers.

On Monday 21 February 1916 there was a disastrous fire at the Heathfield Works. The firm were making waterproof oilskin clothing, using very flammable materials. The fire was discovered at 3.00 a.m. by an overnight maintenance man. He called the fire brigade, who arrived at 3.15. They immediately asked Luton and St Albans brigades for assistance. But even with three engines, the building was completely burnt out within two hours. A company of soldiers arrived and, with local residents, salvaged what they could, storing it in the Silver Cup. The firm hired temporary accommodation at Southdown and resumed partial production a fortnight later.

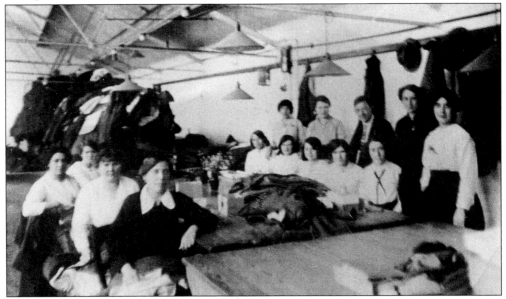

The premises were rebuilt and Abbott, Anderson and Abbott continued to occupy them until 1964, when the firm was acquired by Edward MacBean and Co. of Glasgow and all production work was transferred to Scotland. This picture shows the staff at work in the late 1920s. The new fire station now occupies part of the site.

The Old House, Leyton Road, in 1979. The building dates from Tudor times, with later additions. It was The Bull Inn until 1860. The landlord from about 1830 was Henry Oldaker: he had been a huntsman until a riding accident forced him to retire. He still retained a great interest in horses and in 1839 organised a steeplechase from Friars Wash to Harpenden Common. Among the seven riders was Captain Becher, of the Aintree Becher's Brook fame. He was a regular visitor to The Bull and had a parlour trick which he enjoyed performing. He would leap up the wall and could run a complete circuit around the room without falling.

The rear of the house, c. 1880. Henry Oldaker organised regular annual race meetings on the common from 1848. He retired from The Bull in about 1856 and went to live in St Albans, although he remained Clerk of the Course until his death in 1874. A year or two after he left, The Bull became a private house. The races continued until 1914. The Old House was recently offered for sale at well over half a million pounds.

Bennetts, c. 1895. John Bennet-Lawes the elder, father of the agriculturist, inherited Bennetts in 1789. He had also inherited Rothamsted Manor House from his uncle six years earlier, but allowed his aunt to continue living there until she died. Meanwhile John Lawes the elder lived at Bennetts when he was in Harpenden. He was a London attorney and a friend of the Prince Regent. He used to bring the Prince to Harpenden to hunt and erected extensive stabling at the house for the Prince's horses, nearly bankrupting his family in the process. He died in 1822 leaving Bennetts to his daughter Marianne.

Bennetts on 12 December 1983. In 1847 Marianne Warde returned to Harpenden with her five children after a difficult divorce and took up residence at Bennetts. She was the elder sister of John Lawes, founder of the laboratory. Known as Lady Warde, she lived there until her death in 1891. She was a great supporter of the British School and gave it much practical help. When she died Bennetts was let. For a few months in 1915 it was a private convalescent home for Belgian soldiers. The Royal British Legion bought the building in 1959.

Food and drink has been served at buildings on this site for the past sixty-five years. Mary-Ellen's tea rooms opened in 1932 and are still remembered with affection. When Miss Finnie, the proprietor, retired in 1968 the premises were rebuilt. The Inn on the Green, as seen here, opened in June 1972. It is remembered for serving huge roast turkey legs. This building was demolished in 1992 and the present Inn on the Green built.

Amenbury Lane corner, as painted in 1860, many years before Avenue St Nicholas was built, blocking the view of the Parish Church. Amenbury Lodge now stands on the site. There is a local tradition, related years ago by elderly residents, that Amenbury Lane got its name from a gentleman who lived near the Congregational chapel there. He was noted for the enthusiasm with which he shouted 'Amen' at the end of prayers. His surname was Bury: hence 'Amen'Bury.

Four
Kinsbourne Green
and Luton Road

In the years before the First World War, Kinsbourne Green was a small hamlet nearly two miles north of Harpenden, which effectively stopped at Sun Lane. Luton Hoo was about two miles to the north. The farms around Kinsbourne Green were part of the Luton Hoo Estate and many of the men worked at the Hoo farm. The Hertfordshire Hunt kennels, built in 1866, were on the edge of the Common and the hunt servants lived in cottages nearby. The hounds were exercised across the Common each morning and evening. Sir Julius and Lady Wernher had bought the Hoo in 1903: they took a benevolent interest not only in their workers, but in the people of the hamlet generally. On one occasion, when a cottager's young daughter was seriously ill, Lady Wernher sent her a pint of full cream milk and a fresh egg each day until she was better. They also had erected a corrugated iron hut, just north of the Fox, for use as a Community Hall. Known as the Wernher Room it was very well used for many years, finally being demolished after the Second World War. The Common was covered with heather and bracken and was, in those far off days, the haunt of larks and nightingales. One lady remembers being taken out in the late evening, as a very young child, to see the glow-worms. There was a flock of sheep there: the shepherd lived in a cottage near Annables Farm. During the Second World War the hunt moved to Houghton Regis and the kennels were used as an Ordnance Depot. The Common was ploughed: too rough for conventional tractors to cope with, a steam plough team with two traction engines was used.

The Harrow in the early years of the century. The building was greatly extended in 1980 and became a Beefeater Restaurant. John Deacon was a carrier, running daily between Luton and St Albans. Before bus services started, just after the First World War, he often carried a passenger or two.

The Methodist church at Kinsbourne Green was built in 1856. In 1931 a school hall was added at right angles across the back. The building seen here was in poor condition in 1949 and the members wanted to build a new one. But planning laws would not allow new building on the main road; this chapel was taken down and a new chancel added to the schoolroom, but set back a few feet from the road. It opened on 18 February 1951.

The Pleasance in December 1931, one of the areas of north Harpenden developed by Jesse Catton, photographed by Jack Shearman, one of the first residents. Jesse Catton was a Norfolk man, who moved to London and became a builder. He started to develop the Roundwood Estate in 1910. Ten years later he began the Ridgewood Estate and came to live in one of his houses. The centre of the Pleasance was used as allotments for many years: the bungalows there were built in the '70s.

Kinsbourne Green, c. 1965. The A1081, then the A6, runs diagonally across the picture. To the east of it is Bedfordshire. It is part of the Luton Hoo Estate and is in the green belt. Behind the Pavement shops, which were built in 1937 opposite the Harrow, are Perry's greenhouses. They closed in 1968 and Kinsbourne Close was built on the site. At the bottom of the picture is Kinsbourne Poultry Farm. It closed in the late '60s and Derwent Road and Tintern Close were built there. The road being made at the bottom centre is Shepherds Way, later to fill the field to the right. On the extreme right is The Pleasance; the centre was then being used as allotments.

Six cottages in Roundwood Lane for sale in October 1975. The board said that they were available for modernisation. The site had planning permission for four detached houses. The cottages had been bought as a block before, in 1936, when they were described as 'a sound investment' producing a total income of £114 8s per year. They each had two rooms upstairs and two downstairs. Water then came from one outside stand pipe, which served all six cottages. Each cottage had an earth closet in the back garden.

They were, on this occasion, bought as a block and completely modernised, presenting a very smart appearance in February 1977.

The Old Bell area, c. 1905, looking across the Luton Road from a spot that is now a Hillside Road garden. The Nickey Line bridge is just off the picture to the left. The pair of houses with their backs to us were demolished in 1974 when the site was cleared to build a block of flats, named Bridge Court. The gap between these and the solitary house is the area later covered by the buildings in the picture below. The wood on the horizon is the Round Wood, which gives the district its name.

The eastern side of the road at the Old Bell in 1965. G. F. Tuffin in the centre was an electrical contractor, who opened there in 1963. On the right from 1960 was W.D. Steyning, for woodworkers' supplies and general Do It Yourself materials. When he closed in 1967 the building became L.C. Weston's funeral parlour. At the back were Jarvis's workshops. They moved there in 1964. The whole area was demolished in 1989. There are now two large office blocks on the site.

Edwardian houses on the corner of Luton Road and Hillside Road in 1975. They stood to the immediate right of Steyning's shop (see p.51). This area underwent great change around the late '70s. These houses were taken down in 1980 and replaced by a block of flats named Beech Court. Six years earlier similar houses on the other side of Hillside Road had been demolished and Bridge Court and Bond Court flats were built.

Beech Court in February 1983, a few months after completion. The names Beech and Bridge Court are self-explanatory. Bond Court commemorates Captain Kenneth Hills Bond, usually known as 'Gaffer'. He had served in the Sherwood Foresters during the war and came to Harpenden in 1927. He was a member of the Urban District Council from 1958 until his death in 1976 and its chairman in 1965. He was well known for his hobby: he was a Punch and Judy man, and made all the puppets himself.

The Arch, carrying the Nickey Line over the Luton Road, was built in 1875, wide enough for two railway tracks. In the event, only one was laid, so there was room for an earth embankment across the top to ease the gradient. This is the view through the bridge looking north in about 1900: the houses there now were built in 1904.

The Nickey Line was closed to passenger traffic in 1947 and closed altogether in June 1979. Three years later it was announced that the bridge was to be taken down, but later it was decided to keep it, as part of the Nickey Way footpath, which opened in December 1985, giving walkers a safe crossing of the main road. In 1995 the embankment and trees were removed, the path relaid, and railings fitted for better safety.

Roundwood Park School, c. 1975. The school opened on 7 September 1956 with 179 pupils and 10 staff, including the headmaster, Mr Arthur Foxwell. Extensions were built in 1970 increasing the capacity to 850 pupils. The original buildings are the three blocks at the back. The building to the right of the path, just below the aircraft wing strut, is Roundwood Junior School, which opened a year before the senior school.

Always well used, changing patterns of education placed even greater emphasis on the library as a resource centre. As the school grew, the existing library was too small and overcrowded. It was greatly extended in 1992 and is seen here just before the official opening.

On 6 April 1992 Suzanne Bowd, headgirl, tied a bunch of colourful green and yellow ribbons to the door.

Then, Heather du Quesnay, Director of Education for Hertfordshire, cut them to formally open the library. Haydon Luke, headmaster, and Sheila Brandreth, school librarian, look on, happy to see the completion of many months planning.

The Embassy in Luton Road was Harpenden's third cinema. Captain Frederick Webb, the owner, was Australian: the cinema was called the Austral when it was opened in 1935 by Sir Halley Stewart. He was given a silver model of a kangaroo as a memento. The earlier cinemas were the White Palace, opened on the corner of Amenbury Lane in 1913 and the Regent, opened in 1933 where Waitrose is now.

The sign outside said, 'See the big pictures on the big screen'. It *was* big: compare it to the size of the six foot tall man standing there. The wide panoramic screen was installed in 1953

Until the Public Hall opened in the autumn of 1938 the Embassy, with 870 seats, had the greatest seating capacity of any building in Harpenden. A public meeting was held there on Sunday 1 May 1938 to consider the varied plans drawn up for converting the Red House into a hospital, following Sir Halley Stewart's death on 26 January 1937 (see p.90).

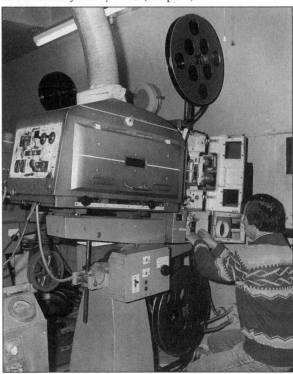

The projectionist setting up his equipment in October 1983, the month the Embassy closed. In the '30s and '40s, Captain Webb also owned the Chequers cinema in St Albans. To cut costs, he used to hire only one copy of the newsreels: when it had been shown at the Chequers, it was put on the bus to Harpenden, collected at the stop outside the cinema by an usherette and rushed up to the projection room. Apparently, with careful timing, the scheme worked.

St Helena's College, c. 1905, was a small select school for young ladies, built in 1897. Some of them were boarders. The school appears to have closed at about the end of the First World War. In 1920 the building was bought for £3,100 and after a central heating and domestic hot water system had been installed, it became Harpenden's Nursing Centre, part of its memorial to those who died during the Great War.

A corner of the studio, which was the building to the right of the house above. Art was an important part of a young lady's education when the school was founded.

Ogglesby's Garage in Luton Road: at the top, as it was in 1955 when Raymond Ogglesby transferred his motor engineering business here from Southdown, and below that, a year later, when he had completely transformed the site. From 1929 this had been the depot for Comfy Cars, Harpenden's own bus company. In 1930 they reached an agreement with Green Line Coaches, whereby seven Green Line vehicles were housed here each night. When, later, Green Line took over Comfy Cars, these premises were used by Car Trailers Limited.

Comfy Cars started running buses between Luton and St Albans in about 1921. Their first base was at the bottom of Station Road, but in 1925 they moved to Vaughan Road, seen here, with a depot next door to Kingston House Mowers. The site is now a restaurant.

Big Car Comfort without the Expense

Phone:
HARPENDEN 124

Write or call—
2 STATION ROAD, HARPENDEN

BE INDEPENDENT

of the railway; taste the joys of the open road with the hedgerows slipping past, and the everchanging view around. To enjoy this independence thoroughly one must have a

COMFY CAR

These are not camouflaged lorries, but first-class touring cars, capable of carrying 20 passengers anywhere in deep-cushioned ease and no loss of time.

LONDON OR LAND'S END

Whether you are going to Town to shop or dance, or 150 miles away to the seaside, ask your friends to come along.

MAKE UP A PARTY

If you get 20 it will be as cheap as the 3rd class railway fair, and—what a difference!

A 1924 advertisement for Comfy Cars.

Five

Station Road
and the Lea Valley

Station Road was originally known as Stakers Lane; the name changed shortly after Harpenden East Station was opened in 1860. In those days it was a narrow country lane leading to Coldharbour and over Pickford Bridge to Batford. In the early years of this century there was a mere handful of houses on the eastern side of the river, mainly in Batford Road. Batford's development really started after the Second World War. Some houses had been built there between the wars, in Salisbury and Southview Roads, but the outbreak of war stopped any further development. After the war the Urban District Council was under great pressure to provide houses for the men and women returning from the forces and for civilians too. The old Prisoner of War Camp in Common Lane was adapted for temporary housing and as soon as permits could be obtained, new houses were started. The 20 year Development Plan for Harpenden, published by the County Council in 1951, proposed the building of 2,000 new houses in the period, 560 of them at Batford. The pictures on pages 72 and 73 show what progress had been made two years later.

Station Road bridge in the early years of the century, well before road traffic became a problem. In 1967 a subway was cut through the left hand bank to make life easier for pedestrians. It was not always easy for motors. On Saturday 5 July 1941 a lorry carrying a concrete mixer was jammed there for several hours. It was eventually released when a number of 'heavy people' were persuaded to climb up on the bonnet and sit there: their combined weight lowered it sufficiently for it to be slowly driven through.

Harpenden Dairies and the new post office in 1928. Harpenden Dairies was a co-operative society of eleven local farmers, selling their milk direct to the public. They delivered an average of 4,000 pints a day. These premises were redeveloped in 1930, with a sparkling new shop next to the post office.

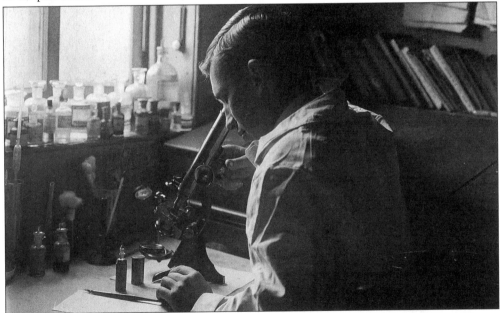

Frederick Norman Gingell, the manager and secretary of the Dairies, in his laboratory. He was very strict in matters of purity and cleanliness and carried out regular tests. Mr Gingell was the originator of the school milk scheme in the 1930s. As a manager of Victoria Road schools he became aware that children from outlying districts were going long periods without nourishment. He arranged with a glass manufacturer to supply small bottles and the school milk scheme was born. It was very quickly taken up nationally.

The forewoman at the Dairies in about the mid-20s, with a mechanical churn lift. This size churn contained about 17 gallons of milk and was very heavy.

Henry Salisbury and Son, builders, developed the Arden Grove Estate during 1906. A few years later they were building the Manland Estate (see p.67). Henry and his wife Susan moved into no. 1 on its completion and lived there until his death in 1923. Susan died four years later. Arthur Lambie then ran his dental practice there until 1956. There was a long garden, stretching up to Station Approach. The house was demolished in 1961 and the shops of Harding Parade built on the site. They opened in 1963.

After wartime service as a sergeant in the Royal Army Medical Corps throughout the North African and Italian campaigns, James Park came to Harpenden in November 1953 and bought no. 28 Station Road. It had been a chemist's shop for about thirty-five years, run by J. R. Stevenson from 1917 until 1950. James Park died in January 1980; his wife continued to run the shop, but was not able to dispense medicines.

A feature of the shop was the mortar and pestle, an old trade sign for the chemist. Shortly after Mr Park's death, Dr Thomas Whittet, who lived in Harpenden, became Master of the Worshipful Society of Apothecaries. To honour his Mastership and as a memorial to her husband, Mrs Park gave him the sign and it was installed in Apothecaries Hall in Blackfriars' Lane, London.

Harpenden's development began with Milton Road in the 1880s. Seen here in about 1895, the houses were substantial and attractive, but the long stretch of wooden fence does nothing for the road's appearance. This area has been completely renovated in the past few years: it is now Poets Corner, where six of the houses have been transformed into luxury one and two bedroom apartments. It could have been very different. In 1962 a developer wanted to build a ten-storey block of flats in Milton Road. It would have been ninety feet high; the proposal did not receive planning approval.

When Mrs Wilson died in 1926, Rivers Lodge (see p.41) was obviously far too big for the two daughters who remained there. Dennis, the youngest son, who was an architect, designed a house in Top Street Way, which was just being developed, for his sisters. The Misses Theodora and Rhoda Wilson moved in in 1927. This was their view, looking across the gardens of Lower Topstreet Farm and the railway line to the gently rising Common.

In 1894 Captain Alfred Dreyfus of the French artillery was arrested in Paris on a charge of high treason. He was accused of spying for the Germans. The military establishment in France was strongly anti-semitic, and Dreyfus was a Jew. His court martial and subsequent imprisonment on Devils Island still remain a shameful blot on French history. The real culprit was Major Charles Ferdinand Esterhazy. Eventually, afraid of being exposed, he fled to England. From 1911 till 1923 he lived in Harpenden, for a short while at the Elms in Station Road and from 1913 at Holmleigh, Milton Road, seen here in 1923.

Known in Harpenden as the Count de Voilement, Esterhazy lived a secluded life, rarely going out except in the late evening, when he rode his horse across the Common, accompanied by a couple of spaniels. He spent most of his time in his study, surrounded by books on French military history. The windows of his home were bolted, and he was said to sleep with a revolver under his pillow. He died on 21 May 1923 and was buried in the parish churchyard. Three months later *The Daily Express* announced the 'startling discovery of the real identity of the Count de Voilement'.

Picture from a 1913 brochure proclaiming the attractions of the Manland Estate, being developed by Henry Salisbury. Station Road curves away to the right and this house stands at its junction with Manland Avenue. 'The Estate', the brochure said 'is about 500 feet above sea level, standing upon a gravel soil, with an invigorating air. The village and common are about ten minutes walk away: tennis, bowls and golf are all within easy distance. Manland provides an ideal spot for a healthy home'.

Harpenden's population increased by over 6,000 people between the wars. A large percentage of the houses they needed were built on the land between the railway lines, bordered by Westfield Road to the north and Crabtree Lane to the south. This is Jameson Road in February 1929; the house at the bottom is in Clarendon Road.

Harpenden Water Company was formed in 1885, originally to serve the Park View Estate and gradually expanded to cover the whole village. In 1960 it joined the Colne Valley Water Company, in accordance with government policy of grouping water undertakings into larger units. At that time Harpenden had two pumping stations operating with a total yield of 1,250,000 gallons a day. The storage capacity was 480,000 gallons, in these two towers in Shakespeare Road. The one on the right was taken down in about 1969 when an underground reservoir with a capacity of 3,000,000 gallons was brought into use.

Overstone Road seen from the water tower in 1936. At the far end it joins Station Road. The top of the tower is 500 feet above sea level, providing a good viewpoint. On the horizon is Bowers Heath.

Overstone Road at ground level in January 1930, looking towards Station Road. The road was made up three years later.

The lower end of St James Road in January 1932 before the buildings had reached it; there were, at this time, half a dozen houses on each side at the higher end. The houses at the bottom are in Willoughby Road and Hyde View Road is on the left.

Willoughby Road in January 1932. The houses in the distance are in Westfield Road.

A painting by Ernest Hasseldine of the Carisbrooke Estate in 1928, before its development in the coming years by E.C. Jarvis. There were 45 acres of undulating farm land. Carisbrooke Road was the first to be built. A feature of the estate was the absence of straight roads.

A family group in the garden of 17 Grasmere Avenue, *c*. 1934. David Smith, who lent me these photographs, is the boy standing on the right.

The view from Grasmere Avenue in about 1932 looking across the Lea Valley. The two houses, just visible on the extreme left, are in Langdale Avenue.

The northern end of the Batford Estate in 1953. The road going up the hill on the right is Porters Hill. After the war, people were very critical about what they perceived as a delay in house building. Mr Gingell replied that the Council was doing well, considering the limits imposed upon it by shortage of labour and materials. They had, in 1947, 60 houses under construction, which would provide 80 dwellings. Some of them were Duplex houses, built as self-contained flats, but designed to be converted to three bedroomed houses when pressure on housing eased.

The Upper Lea Valley Group was formed in 1971. Its aim was to counter years of neglect and to make the river valley an attractive place once more. One of their first tasks was to repair the broken down weir. This scene dates from about 1974 and shows the early stages of preparation.

The southern end of the Batford Estate in 1953, at the same time as the picture opposite. The road in the centre is Pickford Hill. The glasshouses in the foreground are part of Randalls' nurseries, producing salad crops and flowers for the London market. They were demolished in 1959.

The weir in 1975 showing the work completed and stepping stones in place. Later the Group repaired the sluice a little further up stream. Their continuing work has been rewarded with the establishment in 1995 of a ten acre local Nature Reserve there.

Batford Mill from the south, c.1915. The houses visible beyond are in Batford Road. There was a mill at Batford when the Domesday Book was compiled, but this particular building was erected in 1860. It was a flour mill then; in 1901 it was grinding 200 sacks of flour a week. From 1932 until 1950, Willis Bros. were grinding bones there to make fertiliser. They were followed by Coles Plastics, who remained there until 1979. In their time, the old outbuildings were demolished and new industrial units built on the land in the foreground.

Westfield Road bridge was opened on 18 April 1964 replacing an ancient ford. It was 36 feet wide and cost £10,500. It filled a great need as before it opened Pickford bridge was the only one between East Hyde and Leasey bridge. Thirty years later it needed replacing. The road was closed for seven weeks from the beginning of August 1995 and the bridge relaid.

Six

In Times of War

When war was declared in August 1914, the Territorial Army was immediately mobilised. The North Midland Division, which comprised the Notts and Derby, Stafford, and Lincoln and Leicester Infantry Brigades, was allotted Hertfordshire as its training area. On 21 August, four battalions comprising about four thousand men of the Sherwood Foresters (Notts and Derby Regiment) arrived in Harpenden. Public buildings were requisitioned for them and the soldiers were billeted in cottages and houses throughout the village. Most of their activities took place on the Common: they did their physical training there, had musketry instruction and learnt to use the bayonet. But their training area also included the farm land roundabout. At Thrales End Farm they learnt to cope with barbed wire entanglements. At Sundon, near Dunstable, they dug, and occupied against attack, an extensive trench system. They were inspected on 29 September at Luton Hoo Park by Lord Kitchener and again on 6 October by Lord Roberts, at Sandridge. On 16 November they marched to Harlow, where they dug a defensive trench system in preparation for a possible German landing on the Essex coast. On 25 February 1915 they went to France. Meanwhile the North Staffordshire battalions had arrived in Harpenden. Twenty-five years later, in 1939, soldiers and airmen were stationed here. There was a radar station at Kinsbourne Green and searchlights at Annables, Childwickbury and Mackerye End. The Royal Army Service Corps was at Redcliffe and the Royal Signals had a top secret intelligence centre at Rothamsted. The kennels at Kinsbourne Green were an Ordnance Depot and Luton Hoo was the Headquarters of Eastern Command.

The regimental band leading men of the 6th North Staffordshire Battalion from Rothamsted Park on Tuesday 29 June 1915. The regiment had just been inspected by the Earl of Dartmouth, Lord Lieutenant of their county. He said that he had a very high opinion of the quality and soldierly bearing of the troops before him.

Some of the soldiers had meals at their billets, while others ate at messes in the village. This group is collecting the daily bread ration.

A working party, probably about to dig trenches, judging by their equipment.

A military funeral in February 1915, believed to be of a young North Staffordshire soldier who died of influenza. He was 17 and had joined the Army only $2\frac{1}{2}$ months earlier. He died in the hospital at the Institute, after a few days illness. He was buried with full military honours, escorted by the battalion band. Soldiers of his company fired three volleys over the grave and buglers then played the *Last Post*.

Mrs Helen Bentwich was a Woman's Land Army group leader in Hertfordshire. Her job was to recruit ladies to work on the land, then persuade sometimes reluctant farmers to employ them. In May 1917 she bought a motorcycle. She was shown how to start it and off she went along the Great North Road. She then realised that she didn't know how to stop it: so used her heavy Land Army boots as a brake, dragging them along the ground. In Harpenden, she took over the Hunt kennels at Kinsbourne Green and made them into a hostel for her girls.

'Rosemary', no. 28 Milton Road (now the Abbeyfield home), seen from its garden in 1917. The house had been built in 1908 by Henry Tylston Hodgson of the Welcombe, as a smaller house for his wife to move into after his death. But she died in 1910, eight years before him. In 1915 Mr Hodgson offered it to the Army Officer Commanding in Harpenden, rent free, for use as a hospital. It was much bigger than the Institute, which had been the previous hospital.

Staff and patients enjoying the sunshine in 1915. The lady in front, wearing a tie, is Dr V. Kelynack, Commandant of the Harpenden St John's Voluntary Aid Detachment from 1914/16; Mrs F.M. Oakeshott, Commandant from 1916/19 is in the back row, second from right. In the beginning this was a general hospital, with six wards for medical and surgical cases, an isolation ward, and a small ward for officers. There was a well equipped operating theatre, a dispensary and a surgery for outpatients. The hospital had accommodation for thirty patients.

In 1917 the two wooden huts were erected, providing accommodation, and a recreation room, for a further twelve patients. Meanwhile the hospital had changed its status. It closed in May 1916, when the troops left Harpenden, but reopened in March 1917, when there was a desperate need for auxiliary hospitals to relieve pressure on the big military hospitals. Harpenden was affiliated to the main hospital at Napsbury and acted largely as a convalescent nursing establishment for patients from there.

The walking wounded enjoying the day room facilities in 1917. The hut and its equipment cost about £250, which was provided entirely by donations from the people of Harpenden. The medical side of the hospital was under the control of the Royal Army Medical Corps, assisted by the VAD nurses. Mrs Oakeshott, Commandant of the VAD, managed the catering. 'The varied and appetising menus which they produced from the basic foods supplied by the Army were much appreciated', wrote one grateful patient. The war ended in November 1918 and the last patient left this hospital three months later.

The Memorial Cross was unveiled at 2.30 p.m. on Saturday 9 October 1920 by Lieut-General the Earl of Cavan, supported by a number of dignitaries and witnessed by a large crowd of Harpenden people. Lord Cavan was the Commander in Chief at Aldershot and ADC to King George V. He had started the war in command of the 4th Guards Brigade in France and ended it as Commander in Chief of the British Forces with the Italian armies. Lord Cavan was a local man: he had spent his childhood at Wheathampstead House, which was still his home when army duties permitted.

After the unveiling ceremony the dignitaries went across the road to Bowers House, the home of Dr Blake, where they were entertained to tea. Lord Cavan is in the centre, in uniform. Charles Sibley, the chairman of the Memorial Cross committee, which had been responsible for the whole concept, is the large man on the right, standing behind the seated clergyman.

The Memorial Cross on Remembrance Day, 11 November 1920. At the end of the First World War a public meeting decided that, to honour the dead, 'a cross should be erected of such a durable character as would ensure that their names would be remembered from generation to generation'. Ernest Hasseldine, the designer, and Stanley Salisbury, the architect, went to Cornwall to choose the granite. It came from the Penryhn quarries of John Freeman and Sons and they carved it to Ernest Hasseldine's design. The design is based upon a Celtic Cross: the wheel encircling the cross represents eternity and the central boss indicates the Godhead. The three-cornered knot below it represents the Trinity and the intricate interlaced work on the pillar symbolises Christian unity. The names of the 164 men of Harpenden who gave their lives are inscribed on two gun metal tablets at the base of the Cross.

At the time of the Munich crisis in 1938 when war seemed imminent, the Home Office instructed local authorities that gas masks, which were in store, were to be distributed immediately. On Monday 26 September, the Urban District Council borrowed lady assistants from Rothamsted and various firms to supplement its own staff. They assembled and distributed the masks in the old Public Hall, working late into the night and continued on Tuesday, until everyone had received one. Young Brian Webster is seen being fitted for his. The Air Raid Wardens delivered masks to the elderly and housebound.

The *Compleat Air Raid Warden* drawn by M.A. Watson in 1940 and used as a Christmas card by the wardens of Section E9. The caption reads 'The Compleat Air Raid Warden: to wish you "all clear" for a very merry Christmas and a happy New Year'. The ARP wardens, who were all volunteers, were formed on 24 March 1938 and were allocated to districts. The village was divided into forty-two sectors, each in the charge of a Senior Warden, who lived within his sector.

A public air raid shelter being dug out at Bowers Parade in September 1939. The council had been preparing for war for some time. In September 1938 an announcement suggested that householders should be digging trenches straightaway. A specimen trench was on display in Stewart Road, showing dimensions and methods. Mr A. Watts, the head of Manland School, announced in August 1940 that the school was recommending its children, if they were caught in the open in an air raid, to knock on the nearest door and ask for shelter. He made a public plea for people to let them in.

The warden was urged by the government to consider himself 'the father of his flock'. He was to act as guide, philosopher and friend to his people. In order that wardens could be easily found, they were issued with these badges, to be fixed to their gateposts.

In August 1940 the people of Harpenden agreed to raise 40,000 shillings (£2,000), the cost of a Wellington bomber engine, to be 'presented to the RAF'. This was not a savings scheme: the money was to be donated. On the final Saturday morning the fund was £75 short, but a day of fund raising efforts achieved the target. One event attracted a lot of attention: Karl Dane, who had been a sparring partner to Max Baer, the world heavyweight boxing champion, towed a four ton cattle truck, supplied by his employer, Mr H.G. Ivory, several feet by means of a rope held only by his teeth.

Warships Week, 28 February to 7 March 1942. This was a National Savings week, in which people were asked to lend their money to the government for the duration of the war. Harpenden aimed to save £72,000: enough to pay for a motor torpedo boat. The week was opened on Saturday by Admiral Sir Lionel Halsey and within five minutes cheques amounting to £41,000 had been handed to Mr C.F. Putterill, Chairman of the UDC. The target was passed on Monday. The final total was £196,218: enough to provide three motor torpedo boats. Mr Putterill is seen ready to unveil Friday's total.

In June 1940, immediately after Dunkirk, the Ministry of Defence asked Vauxhall to produce a new type of tank. They were to design it from scratch and have it in production within twelve months. Vauxhall knew nothing about tanks, but rose to the challenge. This is a very early model, being tested in Luton Hoo Park. The tanks were constantly being modified. Important visitors came to see them, including King Peter of Yugoslavia, who lived in Harpenden. He was invited to drive one in the Park and enjoyed himself so much that they couldn't get him out: his schedule ran very late that day.

Later models were tested on a road circuit: up Cutenhoe Road and along Luton Road to Thrales End, sometimes stopping at Green Lawns garage for the crew to have a coffee. A concrete lay-by was built at Thrales End, where the engineers could make any adjustment needed. From there they returned to Vauxhalls via Lower Luton Road. Vauxhalls achieved their target: the tank, named the Churchill, was in production within twelve months. Over 5,500 were delivered to the Army. They left Luton by rail and passed through Harpenden East Station at Batford.

No. 10 Crabtree Lane was the only house in Harpenden to be completely destroyed by bombing. It was hit by a high explosive bomb on the night of Sunday 20 October 1940. Fortunately Julie Hobbs and her young daughter were sheltering under the stairs and escaped injury, although they were badly shocked. They had only moved in six months before. It seems probable that the bomber was aiming at the railway line.

A German aircraft dropped a basket of incendiary bombs over Batford in the early hours of Monday 12 May 1941. The Methodist church roof was burnt out and the communion table badly burnt. Some houses nearby were hit: fortunately the damage was slight and there were no casualties.

The damaged interior. The hall behind the church was undamaged and after a lot of clearing up, services were held there while a temporary roof, which turned out to be rather draughty, was put on the church. That had to serve for a few years, until a permanent repair was possible.

Methodists first met in the Batford area in 1884, when after some years of walking from Coldharbour to the Leyton Road Chapel, Mr and Mrs Josiah Smart found the distance too great for their ageing years. They opened their house for services. The space there was soon inadequate, so a corrugated iron chapel was erected in Coldharbour Lane. In 1900 the present site was bought: this church was opened on 25 January 1905. After the Second World War, Batford was developed with a new housing estate and the church was twice extended: in 1952 and 1972. This picture was taken in 1988.

The Home Guard and Civil Defence services held a combined exercise over a weekend in November 1942. Low flying bombers from the American Air Force took part, giving an added touch of realism to events. Here the Home Guard are attacking the Luton Road railway bridge. The group of experienced observers (and there seem to be plenty of them) were said to have been 'highly pleased with the results'.

In March 1941 a co-operative fruit preservation scheme was formed in Harpenden. The aim was to eliminate waste and ensure that all the fruit grown locally was preserved in one form or another. It worked on the principle that some people had surplus fruit, some could spare part of their sugar ration. Each sold their surplus to the co-operative, which then made jam, which could be bought by the original sellers. With the same aim of preserving fruit, the British Legion bought a home canning kit. Mrs Grant, of the Women's Section, is demonstrating its use in the autumn of 1941.

A civil defence exercise in Rothamsted Park, behind Park Hall, testing their ability to deal with bombing casualties. They were continually training and held frequent exercises. In October 1941 a very realistic one, which also involved civilians, was held around the station and Station Road area, when tear gas was released. Passengers on the two trains which arrived between 5.00 p.m. and 5.30 p.m. were not impressed, as many of them were not carrying gas masks. They were said to be 'disinclined to leave the station'.

During the war there was a large and varied collection of buildings behind Park Hall. 'Temporary' garages were erected for ambulances and huts for the greatly expanded wartime fire brigade. They were all demolished in 1993 when the ground was cleared for Harpenden's new Town Hall. The bulldozer in the foreground of this picture, taken in September 1973, is digging out the foundations for the new Sports Hall, which opened in 1975.

In 1930 Sir Halley Stewart gave his home, the Red House, to Harpenden for use as a hospital after his death. He died in 1937. A plan was prepared to build a hospital annexe and use the Red House as a nurses' home, with one room for an electric massage room. Funds were raised and building of the annexe began. The plans were complicated when the Army requisitioned the house in 1939, but after intervention by the Ministry of Health, the Army released it in May 1941. The hospital was opened on Saturday 27 September 1941 by Lady Beatrice Stewart, Sir Halley's daughter-in-law, pictured centre.

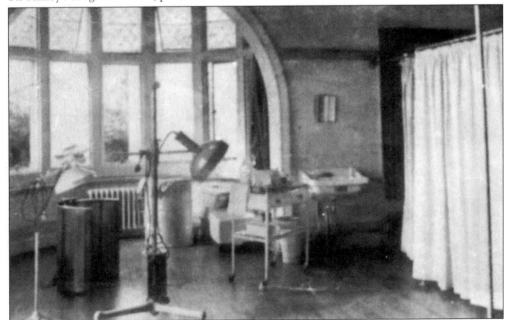

The electric massage room seen here in 1942 was in the main house, immediately to the right of the entrance hall. In its first eleven months, 4,508 treatments were given to 1,212 patients. Five years later, now known as the physiotherapy department, 7,415 treatments were given in a full year and 614 new patients were enrolled.

Part of the crowd at the opening ceremony. The hospital replaced the Nursing Centre at Luton Road. The Red House was much bigger: it had ten bedrooms for nurses, three bed-sitting rooms for sisters and Matron had a sitting room and bedroom. The hospital wing had a maternity unit, with a seven-bed ward and three private wards. There was also a general medical section, with, for some reason that was not explained, an eight-bed ward for women, and a two-bed ward for men. There were also three private wards.

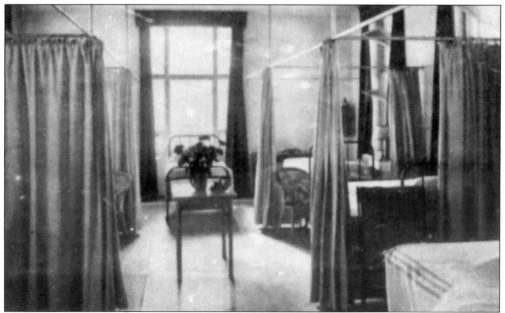

A general ward, 1941. In the days before the National Health service, treatment was not free. People either belonged to a contributory hospital insurance scheme or paid for private beds. In the hospital's third year, 446 patients were admitted: 114 to private wards and 332 to general wards. There were 222 maternity, 126 surgical and 98 medical cases. In 1948 the hospital was nationalised and became part of the National Health Service.

Holidays at Home Week, 5 to 13 August 1944, had a double purpose: to provide a holiday atmosphere for war-weary people and to raise funds for the hospital and the Service Men's Comfort fund. There were many events during the week. On Saturday there was a combined show in the Public Hall, of flowers, fruit and vegetables and handicrafts. At 4.00 p.m. the exhibits were auctioned outside by Bert Goode. He was a member of the Good Companions, a group of local businessmen formed to raise funds for the hospital. This bull calf was sold several times and alone raised £33. The whole week raised £2,122.

VE Day, Tuesday 8 May 1945. All over Harpenden, indeed all over the country, people celebrated the end of the war in Europe. Effigies of Hitler were hanged and then burnt on large bonfires across the village. This is at Southdown. The church bells were rung for a United Service of Thanksgiving at St Nicholas church. Harpenden Hall was floodlit. Soldiers at the Batford Prisoner of War camp added to the festivities by firing Very flares throughout the night.

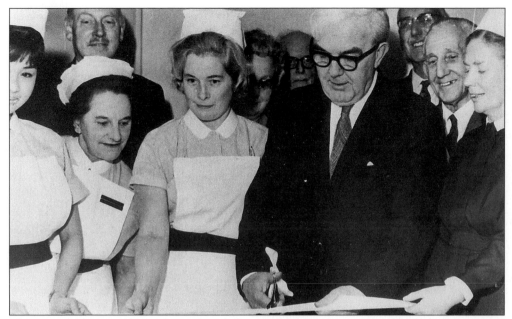

The Hospital League of Friends was founded in 1956. It raised money to provide equipment and amenities which were not available from official sources. In 1964 they provided a Day Room, and, in October 1967, a building extension, seen here being opened by Lord Hill of Luton, a Harpenden resident, who is still remembered as the wartime Radio Doctor. From left to right are: Lorna Roberts; Professor H. Stewart, League President; Doris Petrie; Elizabeth Knowles; unknown; Alf Addison; League Secretary; Lord Hill; unknown; Ernest Ackroyd, Chairman of the UDC; Julia Blanche, Matron.

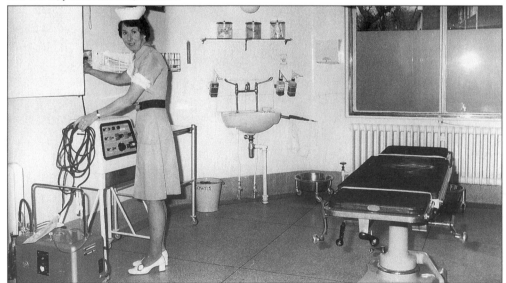

Mrs Rosemary Smith, theatre sister from 1971 until 1990, seen in the theatre on 12 December 1979. She is preparing a defibrillator, a machine used to control the heart during an operation. The whole hospital system is currently undergoing a reorganisation. Harpenden is now known as a community hospital. The theatre is still used; twelve surgeons operate there on day surgery cases.

Hospitals remind me of mortality. Here we have two funerals, with half a century between them. Lieut-Colonel Edward Durnford was born in 1833. A veteran of the Crimean War (1853/56), he and his wife lived at Rothamsted Lodge, the Rothamsted Dower House: he was distantly related to Sir John Lawes. Lt Col Durnford was for many years a manager of the British School.

He and Allen Anscombe, founder of the store, ran a savings bank there, encouraging the children to save by paying $4\frac{1}{2}$ per cent interest. When he became chairman of the newly elected School Board in 1894, its members refused to sanction more than $2\frac{1}{2}$ per cent. Lt Col Durnford died on 30 January 1927 and was taken to the grave on the parish bier.

Eric Morecambe and his wife, Joan, came to live in Harpenden in May 1961. In November of that year, he and Ernie Wise appeared at the Prince of Wales Theatre in their first, of many, Royal Variety Shows. This oil painting, which captures Eric in an unusually serious mood, was presented to him by George Anthony Roe, the local artist, in October 1970.

Eric Morecambe (real name Bartholomew) was in partnership with Ernie Wise from 1939 until his untimely death in 1984. St Nicholas church was far too small for all who wished to attend the funeral on 4 June, so the service was relayed to the hundreds of people outside who had gathered to pay their respects to a much loved comedian and local resident.

The Parish Church of St Nicholas and part of the churchyard, seen from the west, *c.* 1970. There has been a church here since the twelfth century: it was a chapel of ease to St Helen's, the mother church at Wheathampstead and it was there, until 1319, that the Harpenden dead had to be buried. In that year a Papal deed allowed burials to take place in St Nicholas' churchyard. It was difficult to carry bodies to Wheathampstead, particularly in bad weather, because of 'floods and other dangers of the roads'.

This is the oldest gravestone remaining in the churchyard. It commemorates Thomas Law who died on 13 March 1715 in his thirty-third year. The stone is decorated with a skull and crossbones, not because he was a pirate, but as a sign that death comes to us all. On the left is an hourglass, showing that time is running out, and on the right, a pick and shovel, the gravediggers' tools.

Seven
The Daily Round

A hundred and fifty years ago most of the men in Harpenden were working on the land. Others were occupied in providing the community with food, drink and clothing, or supplying work tools and equipment. Some made and maintained various forms of transport. The women and children were mostly employed in straw plaiting and the hat trade. Now patterns have changed. Some jobs have changed beyond all recognition, some have gone for good. In 1997, over half of the working population of just over twelve thousand people are commuters, mainly to London. About one per cent work on the land.

Charles Martin was a recognised authority on well boring and water supply. He established his firm in Amenbury Lane in 1900. He did a lot of work for local water authorities, Luton and Hitchin among them and undertook water supply for estates all over the country. This job is at Hatfield, in about 1910 where he bored to a depth of 400 feet.

Haymaking on an unidentified Harpenden farm in the later years of the last century. In the days before mechanisation, haymaking was one of the jobs that needed a lot of people. Note the cart on the left, being pulled by an ox, not a horse.

Field's Hat Factory at Grove Road, *c.*1890. The firm had started at Heathfield Lodge (see p.42) and came here in 1883. In 1927 they moved into a new, purpose-built factory in Kingcroft Road and remained there until 1935 when the firm closed because of the ill health of the owner. The left hand side of these premises was demolished a few years ago, making space for the entrance to Westminster Court.

At the Chelsea Flower Show, *c.* 1922. Standing between King George V and Queen Mary are James MacDonald and his son Harold, grass specialists of Station Road. James MacDonald founded the firm in 1890; it eventually became the only firm in the country devoting its whole time to research and practical work on grasses. They exhibited regularly at the Chelsea Flower Show and received royal patronage on several occasions, including work on the Sandringham Estate. The firm closed when Harold retired in 1952.

Harpenden's first street lights were lit by gas: in 1888 there were 47 of them. Electricity came to the village in 1923, but was mainly used for domestic purposes. In 1933 the Council's street lighting contract was to be renewed. Gas and electricity competed strongly, each company putting up specimen lights in selected places. Gas won and was awarded a ten-year contract. There were to be 350 lamp standards in all. The new contract made the seven lamplighters redundant: the new lamps were controlled by automatic clocks.

During 1927 the Urban District Council laid a new stormwater drain through the village from Kinsbourne Green to the gravel pits at Southdown. There had long been problems with flooding, especially at the Old Bell, the steepest part of the valley. The work started with a one foot wide pipe at Kinsbourne Green, increasing to a three feet diameter at its end and cost about £3,500. As part of the project the Cock Pond was filled in and the small stream running from it incorporated in the drainage system.

The First World War trophy, a German field gun, which stood on this Green, was removed to the Council yard while work was being done. It was never brought back. There was a fairly strong peace movement in Harpenden at the time, which may have had something to do with it. In October 1931, over half the adult population signed the International Declaration in favour of World Disarmament organised by the League of Nations. During the Second World War, the gun went for salvage.

Monsieur François Carofe, the onion man from Brittany, in Leyton Road in 1961. He has nearly a hundredweight of onions on his bicycle. The custom of Breton farmers bringing their onions to England started at the end of the last century. The trade was suspended during the last war, but resumed immediately afterwards. Monsieur Carofe came to Harpenden for many years, selling from door to door, until the annual visits of the farmers died out in the '60s.

Benjamin Rowe married in 1907 and came to Harpenden shortly afterwards. He and his wife took over John Iron's bakery at 64 High Street (see p.23) and in his early days he started work at 4 a.m. and finished at 9 p.m. The firm's advertisements in 1923 said 'Daily deliveries by motor'. This is believed to be his first motorised vehicle. He was still driving the delivery van until shortly before his death in 1969 at the age of 87, although the business was then being run by his son, Norman.

The watercress beds at East Hyde in April 1955. Although the wild watercress plant was known, and had been gathered, since at least 1748, commercial growing in Hertfordshire is believed to have started in 1812. Certainly by 1820 watercress from the county was regularly on sale in the London markets.

Watercress needs large quantities of pure water, with a carefully controlled flow through the shallow beds. The chalk streams of Hertfordshire were ideal and cress was grown all along the Upper Lea at East Hyde, Batford, and Castle Farm. It is an all year round crop and can be harvested up to twelve times a year.

The cress was packed in flat oblong osier baskets, as seen here at Waterend Lane ford at Redbourn, c. 1900. These were sent by rail to the markets in London and the Midlands; large quantities went from both Harpenden East and the Midland stations. Cress is no longer cultivated in the Upper Lea. Increasing demand for water has lowered the water table and it is no longer economic to grow.

William Frost came to Harpenden from Norfolk in 1927 and established his basket-making business here. He bought a five acre plot of land alongside the River Lea, just south of Piggottshill Lane, where he planted thousands of willow 'sets', which grew into osiers, the raw material of his trade. The willow shoots (osiers) were cut and kept under water for a couple of days and then put through the 'brake' to strip off the bark. Here in about 1930, his wife and sons are preparing some shoots for him.

John Lawes came down from Oxford in 1834, aged twenty, and with his mother took up residence at Rothamsted Manor, which he had inherited on his father's death twelve years before. Interested in chemistry, he had one of the best bedrooms set up as a laboratory, much to his mother's annoyance. A casual remark by Lord Dacre of Kimpton Hoo concentrated his attention on chemistry applied to agriculture. On 1 June 1843 he appointed Joseph Henry Gilbert to assist him. This barn, long since demolished, is where they carried out their first experiments and where the Rothamsted Experimental Station began.

The Station's Golden Jubilee was celebrated in 1893. In the presence of a large crowd of dignitaries, most of whom had come by special train from St Pancras, the eight-ton boulder of Shap granite was unveiled, amongst many congratulatory speeches. Sir John Lawes was presented with his portrait, painted by Hubert Herkomer RA. It now hangs in the library at Rothamsted. Sir John is seen responding to the many congratulations offered to him and Dr Gilbert.

104

Official guests at the centenary celebrations in 1943. On a tour of Broadbalk are, left to right: Sir John Russell, director of the station from 1912; James Russell Moffatt, the farm agent; Lord Radnor, chairman of the Lawes Agricultural Trust; Robert S. Hudson, Minister of Agriculture; and Dr William Ogg, who became director later that year when Sir John Russell retired.

The Queen visited Rothamsted on Friday 30 July 1993, the 150th anniversary year, and delighted everyone by announcing that she had agreed to become Rothamsted's Patron. After a tour of the buildings and farm, during which she talked to staff and their families, the Queen unveiled a plaque to commemorate her visit and to mark the launch of Rothamsted International, an initiative by Rothamsted to foster and increase their international links. With the Queen is Professor Trevor Lewis, Head of Rothamsted.

In the early days, goods traffic, especially coal, was more important to the railways than passengers. Most stations had goods yards, where the competing coal merchants had their sheds. These are two Harpenden coal dealers at about the turn of the century. The goods yard was not closed until 1964 and is now the station car park. In the years immediately after the Second World War, when coal was scarce, C.J. Williams was selling peat blocks as a substitute at 17s 6d ($87\frac{1}{2}$p) per hundred.

The miniature garden on the centre platform at Harpenden station in July 1950. Foreman S. Buckingham, who was one of the railwaymen responsible for building it, is pointing out to a couple of passengers the goldfish in the ornamental pond. The gardens were removed in about the mid-'60s.

Signalmen Alf Morgan, on the left, and Keith Howard on duty in the Harpenden Junction signal box near Hollybush Lane, *c.* 1965. The line diagram on the wall behind them shows the Nickey Line forking away from the mainline. The Nickey Railway to Hemel Hempstead opened in 1877. It closed to passenger traffic in 1947 and closed completely in 1979. The signal box was removed in 1981.

The level crossing and gatekeeper's cottage at Leasey Bridge in August 1963. This line, a branch of the Great Northern Railway, was opened in 1860 and went from Hatfield to Luton, passing through Batford. It closed on 24 April 1965. The track has been removed and the Upper Lea Valley walk created along its route.

This portrait, elegantly posed by Frederick Thurston in about 1885, is of three sisters: Louise, Amy and Maggie White, whose daily round was spent at home, engaged in needlework and other ladylike pursuits.

Eight
High Days and Holidays

Harpenden has long had a reputation for doing things well. National and local events have been celebrated with enthusiasm, from Queen Victoria's Golden Jubilee in 1887 to the 1995 celebrations commemorating fifty years since the end of the Second World War. Perhaps the most outstanding festivities were those for the Festival of Britain in 1951. Buildings were floodlit and the whole village was decorated with fairy lights and oriental lanterns. A varied programme of events took place throughout the week. So successful were they that mid-week The Times national newspaper had a half-column report on the activities. The week concluded with a fireworks display on the Common, arranged by Brocks Crystal Palace Fireworks (whose factory was at Redbourn), which attracted a crowd of more than 30,000 people, well over half of them coming from surrounding towns and villages. Harpenden's total population was at the time only 14,244. Various sports have always been well followed. The Herts Advertiser, looking at the sporting scene in 1933, pointed out that the only handicap to even greater involvement was the lack of suitable grounds. To alleviate this problem, the Urban District Council bought Rothamsted Park in 1938, but plans to set out pitches were delayed until after the war. Then there were sites for football, cricket, hockey, tennis, lacrosse, putting, pitch and putt, and quoits. In 1975 the Sports Hall, one of the last works of the Urban District Council, was opened, providing facilities for indoor sports.

A picnic on the Common in about the 1890s, of which nothing else is known. They were probably watching a cricket match.

Queen Victoria's Golden Jubilee on Tuesday 21 June 1887. The day, which was warm and sunny, was celebrated with enthusiasm in Harpenden. The church bells were rung in the early morning. After a service in the Parish Church a large crowd, led by the village band, dressed in new uniforms, paraded to Rothamsted Park, lent for the occasion by Sir John Bennet Lawes.

A little further up the Park, several tents had been pitched and tables laid. More than 2,000 villagers were served a substantial dinner of meat, potatoes and plum pudding. The day's celebrations concluded with a fireworks display on the Common.

The afternoon was devoted to athletic sports, in which large numbers took part. A long course had been prepared and it was well lined with spectators. The man in the left hand picture, standing back, is Sir John Bennet Lawes.

CYCLE PARADE
at Harpenden

There was an equally enjoyable day ten years later for the Queen's Diamond Jubilee on Monday 28 June 1897. A programme of sports was held on the Common and in the evening there was a torchlit cycle parade through the village, with the riders in fancy costume. The day closed with the lighting of a huge bonfire at ten o'clock.

Races were held in the spring on the Common every year from 1848 until 1914, when they were stopped because of the war (see p.44). Race day was a gala day for the village. Everyone who could took a holiday, not only to see the races, but also to enjoy the various side-shows which were set up. So many school children played truant, that after a few years the schools bowed to the inevitable and made race day an official holiday. This picture is from the early 1900s.

A gypsy caravan coming to Harpenden for the fair in September 1931. Large groups of gypsies gathered here for the races and the autumn Statty Fair, and parked their caravans on the Common. The Statty has been known by that name since the last century, although, as far as is known, there does not appear to be any actual statute establishing it.

During the First World War the Admiralty ordered a fleet of thirty-two paddle minesweepers and named them all after racecourses. HMS *Harpenden* was commissioned in April 1918 and served in Home waters and the Baltic until December 1919, when she was paid off at Sheerness. She was then berthed at Harwich for disposal and eventually sold for scrap in 1928.

When the *Harpenden* was broken up, the ship's bell was given to the Right Hon J.C.C. Davidson, MP for the Hemel Hempstead Division, which then included Harpenden. He presented it in 1930 to the Public Library. Mrs J. Henderson-Smith, honorary secretary of the Library, is showing it to a group of young readers. The bell is still there, together with a brief history of HMS *Harpenden*.

Skating on the Silver Cup pond in the early years of this century. It was a natural pond in the last century, but in 1899 it was reconstructed by Sir John Lawes. 2,200 tons of earth were dug out and the hole then concreted, creating a pond 170 feet long by 134 feet wide. It was 4 feet deep in the middle and held, when full, 260,000 gallons of water. It was a popular spot, used for paddling, skating and sailing model boats. Condemned in 1969 as a health hazard, it was broken up in January 1970.

1ST ANNUAL SHOW BY HARPENDEN ALLOTMENT HOLDERS AUGUST 1910

The first Horticultural Society was formed on 18 May 1889. It flourished for some years, then lapsed. It restarted in 1910 and this picture is of the first annual show held in the Old Public Hall in August. Sitting on the table is Colonel Durnford (see p.94). Next to him on the right is Edwin Grey of Rothamsted. The lady is Lady Carlisle and on her right is her husband, Sir Hildred Carlisle, MP for the division. On the stage is the Harpenden String Orchestra, conducted by Fred Blake.

A Grand Fair was held on the Common in June 1923, organised by Mrs Laura Nott, to raise money for the Harpenden Memorial Nursing Centre in Luton Road and the West Herts Hospital at Hemel Hempstead. It was opened by the Earl and Countess of Strathmore, from St Paul's Waldenbury, who were very much in the news. Only a few weeks earlier on 26 April, their daughter, Elizabeth (now the Queen Mother) had married the Duke of York. About 20,000 people attended the fair, which raised just over £2,000. This is the view from the Old House (see p.44).

The Green at Southdown, decorated for the coronation celebrations of King George VI on 12 May 1937. On the day, schoolchildren created intricate patterns while dancing round the maypole.

Advertising, 1921 style. Sandwich-board men were a common sight on the streets of towns in the '20s. By walking around the town centre all day, they showed the message to many people. These men are advertising a programme of classical tableaux, shown at the Public Hall in April 1921. Now completely out of fashion, tableaux were popular in the early years of the century. The programme tells a story, not as a moving play, but in a series of 'living pictures'.

The Story of Perseus was shown in sixteen scenes; this picture is of the first scene, in which King Acricius turns his back on his daughter and baby grandson, after ordering their exile, because an oracle had warned him that his grandson would be the cause of his death. The cast, who had all made their own costumes, stood completely still while a narrator told the audience, in verse, what each scene represented.

116

In March 1933 the Harpenden Women's Conservative Association held their annual social in the Old Public Hall. During the evening a short cabaret, entitled Oddities was performed by pupils of the Harpenden School of Dancing in Vaughan Road (see p.32). They were led by the principal of the school, Kathleen Gillow, seen on the far right of the top picture, and in the middle of the other, and performed several song and dance numbers. Wilfred Busby, Miss Gillow's fiancé, assisted with some songs, poking gentle fun at the Urban District Council.

The Ambrose Concert Party, c. 1930. They were all on the staff of the National Children's Home printing school. They had a wide repertoire and were very popular at local concerts. From left to right: W. Allgood; A. Pluck; B. Thom; W. Milligan; A. Bird; and at the piano, Miss Howe.

The Silver Jubilee of King George V and Queen Mary in May 1935 was celebrated with a carnival procession through the High Street. The Loch Ness monster, led on a piece of string by E.F. Arnold, a member of Toc H, attracted a lot of attention. The legs, which are just visible, are of other Toc H members who provided the means of propulsion.

Another carnival two years later, for the Coronation of King George VI on 12 May 1937. Fourteen year old Jean Alexander, of East Common, won first prize in the decorated bicycle section for her portrayal of Queen Boadicea. The horses behind, looking on, are ridden by members of the Legion of Frontiersmen.

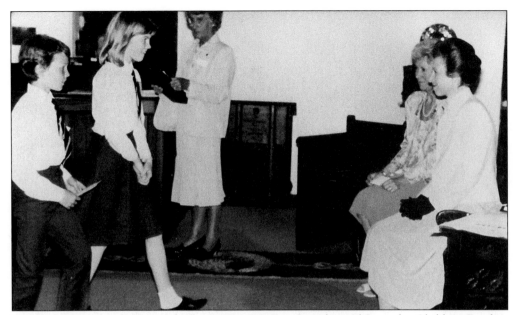

Princess Anne visited Harpenden on 8 May 1987 as President of Save the Children Fund to receive donations from all the schools in Harpenden. The meeting was held at St George's, which has been a supporter of the Fund ever since 1926. Seen here presenting their school purse, are the representatives from High Beeches. The children there had raised money by holding a 'mufti' day, on which they paid not to wear school uniform. Presenting the purse are the oldest girl and the youngest boy in year 6, Andrea Fryer and Neil Jaggard. Sitting with Princess Anne is Mrs Joan Bartholomew, local President of the Fund.

Princess Diana in Milton Road on 23 September 1987. She was visiting Spelthorne St Mary Home for Women: a big event for Harpenden and the local papers, but fairly routine for the nationals. Nevertheless, the visit achieved national coverage in many of them. Andrew Clarke, from Cheshire, visiting his sister in Harpenden, was about to take a photograph of the Princess, when she stopped to speak to him, saying that she had the same camera. Acting on the spur of the moment, he kissed her hand, and gave the pressmen there an unusual picture.

St George's Co-educational Boarding School moved from Keswick to Harpenden in 1907, taking over the empty buildings in Carlton Road which had been used for the previous two years by the boys of the United Services College. This is the first school sports day there in 1908.

Roundwood Park School was built in the mid-1950s to relieve the pressure on Manland School (now Sir John Lawes) caused by Harpenden's rapidly growing population. It opened on 7 September 1956. Here we see one of the races in their first sports day in 1957.

Harpenden Cricket Club's records date from 1894, although there is evidence that cricket was being played fairly regularly on the Common from 1880. This is the team of 1922. Their star players were W.H. Marsh and C.H. Titchmarsh, 2nd and 4th in the middle row. Billy Marsh was a regular member of the side from 1898 until 1923. His best season was in 1906, when he took 116 wickets and also scored 1,102 runs. 'Titch Titchmarsh' played from 1909 until his untimely death at the age of 49 in 1930. He was the club's pre-eminent batsman: in 1913 playing for club and county he scored a total of 4,016 runs, including 21 centuries.

Frederick Gingell owned a plot of land at Coldharbour on the corner of Pickford Bridge, where in 1939 he planted 100 willow trees. In March 1952, some of them were cut down by men from F.N. Skinner's works at Hoddesdon, ready to be made into cricket bats. Frederick Gingell, on the right, was, in his younger days, a keen cricketer himself. He was in the team seen above, sitting on the ground on the left.

Two uses of the Common. Top: the North of the Thames Cross Country Championships on Harpenden Common in February 1938. The course, three times around the Common, was just under seven and a half miles long; 221 runners, representing 23 clubs, took part: the first four were all home in under forty minutes. The Common was a popular *rendezvous* for a drive in the country in the '50s. This is the scene on August Bank Holiday 1955. The UDC were not too happy about the number of cars parked on the Common though.

George Gridley in his workshop in 1953. He had been the woodwork master at Manland School until his retirement in 1951. He first became interested in archery in 1937, and helped to found the Harpenden Bowmen in 1949. He was later elected president of the club. A qualified archery coach, he made all his own equipment. Here he is working on a new bow.

The Harpenden Bowmen, founded in 1949, met on the Rugby Club ground at the end of Overstone Road. Stan Smith, who lent me the photograph, is fourth from the right on the front row; his wife Rene is standing next to him. She was the club's Lady Champion at the time. The Rugby Club moved to a new ground at Hatching Green in 1964 and the land was developed for housing.

In 1951, Hitchin Pageant Year, the Bowmen gave an exhibition at Hitchin Priory, dressed in medieval costume. Without changing, they stopped on the way home at The Royal Oak between Hitchin and Codicote and created some amusement amongst the regulars.

Festival of Britain, May 1951. Enid Webb, wearing a 100 guinea silver and white crinoline, which had originally been worn in a West End production of *The Student Prince*, was crowned Queen of the Revels by Frank Salisbury at the Grand Carnival Ball on Friday night. Her attendants, wearing dresses of gold, were Pauline Bailey on the left and Doreen Deamer. Music was provided by Mantovani's Music Makers, of BBC fame, and relayed to the crowds outside the Public Hall, where there was an impromptu street dance.

On Tuesday evening, members of the Urban District Council led parties of people around the village 'beating the bounds', then returned to the Common for an 'induction ceremony' in which prominent local personalities were led to the ducking stool at the Silver Cup pond. First to go was Councillor Henry Williamson, Chairman of the UDC. This is Councillor Maurice Drake, the youngest member of the Council. He took the precaution of removing his shoes.

On Saturday afternoon there were races through the High Street, a soap box derby for the boys and a hoop race for the girls. There was a pram race for the ladies and a barrel rolling competition for the men. Because of numbers, the barrel race was run in three heats, with the three winners running a final. Competitors had to roll a barrel from The Cock to The George: and it's not easy to get a barrel to run in a straight line. The winner was E.T. Rolt, who won a keg of J.W. Green's Luton beer for his efforts.

A programme of old-time sports was held on Wednesday; those taking part paraded in period costumes from The Cock to their various positions. A boxing ring was set up near the fountain and a series of bouts culminated in a bare-fist fight between 'Farmer' John Tulloch from Redbourn and 'Gentleman' John Brydon of Harpenden. There were no rounds: it was a continuous fight. After about fifteen minutes both contestants looked rather battered, but the fight ended a moment later when 'Farmer' Tulloch was knocked out.

On Thursday evening beside a mammoth camp fire, Gypsy Petulengro, the King of the Romanies, married two of his people, Sophie and Johnny Smith, with eight girls from Westfield as bridesmaids. Petulengro cut the couple's hands, the groom's right and bride's left, and joined them together, so that the blood mingled. He then tied them with a silken cord, in which the bridesmaids had tied knots, representing affection, sincerity, long life, fidelity and the blessing of fertility. When the cord was cut, Johnny leapt over a small fire, followed by his bride, and they then returned hand in hand.

Batford swimming training pool at its official opening in May 1954. On the left is Mrs F.V. Travers, the instructor. Funds were raised locally to build the pool, on land given anonymously before the war by Jesse Catton, founder of the building firm. It was used for many years in teaching youngsters to swim, but eventually suffered from vandalism and became a sandpit.

This car transporter was being driven along the High Street in February 1978 when the leading car slipped its moorings and swung out to the side. It demolished a lamp post and road sign at Station Road corner, opposite the Midland Bank. Police guided the driver to Southdown Road - this part has since been grassed over - where the remaining cars were unloaded. The road was then closed until a crane arrived to remove the front two.

In 1979 the old Elm tree growing in the concourse outside Woolworth's died of Dutch Elm disease. In February 1980 the Harpenden Society organised a street collection, raising money to pay for a new tree, as a way of celebrating the Society's Golden Jubilee. On 27 November 1980 this 25 year old, 30 feet high Norwegian Maple was brought from Surrey by road to be planted in its place. Jarvis the builders, celebrating their 75th anniversary, renewed the brickwork around the tree.

Acknowledgements

I gratefully acknowledge assistance and the loan of photographs from: Mrs J. Bartholomew; Mrs P. Burgin; Mr N. Cantillon, editor of *The Herts Advertiser*; Mrs A. Coburn; I Mr D. Crew, Mrs M. Eggle; Mr M. Ferrara; Miss J. Gingell; Mrs D. Godwin; Mr L. Green; Mrs E. Haines; Professor T. Lewis of Rothamsted; Mr S. Lloyd; Mrs J. Lovatt; Mr H Luke; Mr R. Marshall; Mr P. Moyse; Mrs J. Nette; Mr E. Ogglesby; Mr J. Ollerenshaw; Mrs M. Pigott; Mrs E. Salisbury; Mrs L. Shearman, Mrs M. Skinner; Mr D. Smith; Mr S. Smith; Mrs E. Waldram; and Mrs P. Weatherley.

Thanks to Aerofilms for permission to reproduce nos. 35 and 49; to Mr C. Grabham, Luton Museum and the *Luton News* for nos. 22, 26B, 124A and B, 125A and B, and 126A and B; to Mr L. Casey, curator of Harpenden Local History Society and Mr G. Woodward for freely sharing information; to Mr E. Meadows for permission to use some of his photographs and for copying most of the rest; and to Mrs L. Goucher for word-processing my manuscript. Most of these pictures have been deposited with the Harpenden Local History Society which is always glad to see material of local interest. Lastly, my apologies if anyone's name has been inadvertently omitted.